THE PERFECT PUT-DOWN

by
Eric & Neil & Roger & Carl & Carol
MOSESSON

Illustrated by Tom Eaton

SCHOLASTIC BOOK SERVICES

NEW YORK · TORONTO · LONDON · AUCKLAND · SYDNEY · TOKYO

ISBN 0-590-09940-X

13 12 11 10 9   2 3 4 5 6/8

Printed in the U.S.A.

01

Put Downs

New bride: I've been cooking for ten years.

Mrs. Smith: Then I guess you ought to be ready by now!

Rude boy on a blind date: You could make a good living hiring yourself out to haunt houses.

"If I've said anything to insult you, believe me, I've tried my best."

They call him "Chocolate bar." He's half nuts.

He looks about as comfortable as a centipede with athlete's foot.

He might as well blow out his brains. He's got nothing to lose.

He's such a blockhead, he gets splinters in his fingers every time he scratches his head.

He's a second story man. No one ever believes his first story.

Jim: You know, Sam spends half his time trying to be witty.

Tim: You might say he's a half-wit.

Hank: My mom treats me like an idol.

Frank: What makes you say that?

Hank: She feeds me burnt offerings at meals.

Don: Our dog is just like one of the family.

John: Really? Which one?

Rick: She sure gave you a dirty look.

Dick: Who?

Rick: Mother Nature!

Cindy: I'm disgusted!

Mindy: Why?

Cindy: I stepped on the scale today and it said, "One person at a time please."

Smith was reading insurance tables.

"Say, do you know that everytime I breathe a man dies?"

His friend Jones replied,

"Why don't you use a little mouth-wash now and then."

Bill: Want to lose ten pounds of ugly fat?

Phil: Sure!

Bill: Cut off your head.

Ed: I've changed my mind.

Ted: Thank goodness. Does the new one work any better?

Boy: How do you keep a moron in suspense?

Friend: I don't know, how?

Boy: I'll tell you tomorrow.

Fay: I throw myself into everything I undertake.

Jay: Go dig a deep well.

Tom: When you grow up you're going to be an M.D.

Jerry: Oh?

Tom: Yeah, Mentally Deficient.

One day a really skinny man was walking along when he met a really fat man. The fat man said, "Looks like you've been in a famine." So the skinny man said, "Looks like you caused it."

Mrs. Smith, reading a newspaper: Did you know that a great many accidents occur in the kitchens of our homes?

Mr. Smith: Yes, I know. I've eaten quite a few of them.

Worn-out baby-sitter to a returning parent: Don't apologize for being late. I wouldn't be in a hurry to come home either.

Bill: Last night I met a girl and fell in love at first sight.

Phil: Why don't you invite her to the prom?

Bill: I took a second look.

Randy: Did you fill in that blank yet?

Andy: What blank?

Randy: The one between your ears.

Mrs. Smith: Whenever I'm in the dumps, I get a new hat.

Mrs. Jones: Oh, so that is where you get them.

An angry customer, telephoning her grocer: I sent my little boy for three pounds of nuts and you gave him only two pounds. Are you sure that your scales are correct?

Grocer: Madame, my scales are accurate. Have you weighed your little boy?

Jed: If I saw a man beating a donkey and made him stop, what virtue would I be showing?

Ted: Brotherly love.

Jokes

FAMILY

Little Sally (showing a scale to a little playmate): All I know is you stand on it, and it makes you mad.

Big sister: Eat your spinach; it will put color in your cheeks.
Little sister: Who wants green cheeks anyway?

"Where did I come from?" asked the little ear of corn.
"The stalk brought you," answered its mother.

Mother to father: Baby Charles is such a treasure.
Mean big brother: Yup, let's bury him!

Small brother: What do you call a person who has guests for dinner?
Big sister, hesitantly: A hostess.
Small brother, grinning: No, a cannibal.

Mother: Now, Ann, don't you know you're not supposed to eat with your knife?
Ann: Yes, Mother, but my fork leaks.

Mother: What do you want to take your cod liver oil with this morning, Elmer?

Elmer: A fork.

Father teaching his daughter to drive: Stop on red, go on green, and take it easy when I turn purple.

Sally: I don't like the cheese with the holes in it.

Mother: Don't fuss, dear. Just eat the cheese and leave the holes on your plate.

Worried mother: Why is your report card always so poor?

Tommy: Mom, I can't help it. I don't sit next to any smart kids.

One day Billy came home from school and said to his dad: "There's a special P.T.A. meeting tonight—just you, Mom, my teacher, and the principal."

Mother: Tommie, why did you kick your little sister in the stomach?

Tommie: I couldn't help it, she turned around too quickly!

"Mother," asked Bobby, "is it true that we were dust before we were born?"

"Well, I guess so."

"And is it true that you're dust after you're dead?"

"I guess so," said Mother again.

"Then," said Bobby, "there's somebody either coming or going under my bed."

Betty: I've been helping you, Mommy.
Mother: What have you been doing?
Betty: I licked all the stamps so they'd be ready to be put on your letters.

Little boy: Daddy, Mommy was backing the car out of the garage, and ran over my bicycle.
Father: Serves you right. How many times have I told you not to leave it on the porch?

Mother: What's the matter with your little brother?
Tommy: He's crying because I'm eating my cake and won't give him any.
Mother: Is his own cake gone?
Tommy: Sure, and he cried all the time I was eating that too.

Mother: Aunt Maude will never kiss you goodbye if you have such a dirty face.

Joan: That's what I thought.

Jim's father to Jim: One thing in your favor. With these grades, you couldn't possibly be cheating.

Father: Well, son, how do you like school?

Son: Closed!

Mother: Why do you want to keep this bag of dirt, Tommie?

Little Tommie: It's instant mud pie mix.

Boy: Did your father ever spank you?

Friend: Yes.

Boy: Did your mother ever spank you?

Friend: Yes.

Boy: Who hurt the most?

Friend: I did!

Mother to finicky child at the table: Eat it dear, pretend it's mud.

Susan: Look at that man! He doesn't have any hair at all.

Mother: Shh..., he might hear you.

Susan: Doesn't he know it?

Father: Why did you kick your friend?

Jimmy: I wanted him to go home.

Father: Why didn't you ask him to go home?

Jimmy: That wouldn't be polite.

Little Johnny just returned from his first day of school.

"Tell me, son" asked his mother, "did you learn anything today?"

"A little," answered Johnny in disgust. "But not enough. I've got to go back again tomorrow."

Mother: What are you looking for, Jane?

Jane: Nothing.

Mother: You'll find it in the box where the candy was.

Dad: I'm spanking you because I love you.

Kid: I wish I was old enough to return my love.

A father walked into the living room and saw his son sitting before a blazing fire. This disturbed him very much, because they didn't have a fireplace.

Father was showing Sam the family album and came across a picture of himself and his wife on their wedding day.

"Was that the day Mom came to work for us?" Sam asked.

Father: I broke my son's habit of biting his nails.
Friend: You did—how?
Father: I knocked his teeth out.

Son: Pop, what's a weapon?
Father: It's something you fight with.
Son: Is Mom your weapon?

Mother: Stop asking so many questions. Don't you know curiosity killed the cat?
Jane: Really? What did the cat want to know?

Mother: Sit down and tell me what your school grades are.
Son: I can't sit down. I just told Dad.

"Mother," said little Johnnie, "today our teacher asked me whether or not I had any brothers or sisters, and I told her I was an only child."

"And what did she say?"

"Thank goodness," Johnnie replied.

A father who wants his children to get an education these days may have to pull a few wires; the television wire, the telephone wire, the stereo wire, and the radio wire.

Mother: Well, Joe, how are your marks?

Joe: They're under water.

Mother: What do you mean?

Joe: They're below C level.

Young man: I've come to ask for your daughter's hand in marriage.

Father: You'll have to take all of her, or it's no deal.

Brother: Want to see something swell?

Sister: Sure.

Brother: Hit your head on a baseball bat.

A father took his young son to the opera for the first time. The conductor started waving his baton, and the soprano began her aria. The boy watched everything and finally asked, "Why is he hitting her with his stick?"

"He's not hitting her," answered the father, laughing.

"Well, then," asked the boy, "why is she screaming?"

Father: Didn't you promise me to be a good boy?

Son: Yes, Father.

Father: And didn't I promise you no spending money if you weren't?

Son: Yes, Father. But since I've broken my promise, you can break yours.

Mrs. Smith: Why is Jones pacing up and down like that?

Mr. Green: He's awfully worried about his wife.

Mr. Smith: Why? What's she got?

Mr. Green: The car.

Traffic cop: Lady, you were doing seventy-five miles an hour.

Woman driver: Oh. Isn't that wonderful, and I only learned to drive yesterday.

It was the first day on the job for the pretty blond stenographer just out of business school. Her boss picked up the first of her finished letters and with a sigh said, "You can't spell very well, can you? I see that you have spelled sugar, suggar."

"Oh dear, so I have!" she exclaimed. "Now how do you suppose I left out the 'h.'"

Mrs. Jones to the new hired girl: Have you given the gold fish fresh water, today?

Girl: No, Ma'am. They haven't finished the water I gave them yesterday.

Lady to traffic cop: Does this summons cancel the one I got this morning?

Cooking teacher: And now, girls, for your final examination—eat what you have made.

SCHOOL

Teacher: What is your favorite state?
Sam: Mississippi.
Teacher: Spell it.
Sam: Err...I like Ohio much better.

First student: How were your exam
   questions?
Second Student: They were easy, but I
   had trouble with the answers.

Teacher: Bobby, if you put your hands
   in one pants pocket and found
   seventy-five cents and you put your
   hand in the other pants pocket and
   found twenty-five cents, what would
   you have?
Bobby: I'd have somebody else's pants
   on.

Teacher: You can be sure that if
   Moses were alive today, he'd be con-
   sidered a remarkable man.
Jim: He sure ought to be, he'd be more
   than twenty-five hundred years old.

Teacher: Yes, Sammy, what is it?

Sammy: I don't want to scare you, but Pop said if I don't get better grades someone is due for a spanking.

Professor: What was the outstanding accomplishment of the Romans?

Student: They understood Latin.

Georgie: Teacher, would you scold anybody for something they didn't do?

Teacher: Of course not. But, why do you ask, Georgie?

Georgie: Well, I didn't do my homework.

Laugh, and the class laughs with you.
But you stay after school alone.

Student: I et seven biscuits for breakfast.

Teacher: Ate.

Student: Well, maybe it was eight.

Teacher: Explain the manners and customs of the natives of Borneo.

Pupil: They ain't got no manners and they don't wear no costumes.

Teacher: Tell me the truth, now. Who really did your homework?

Johnnie: My father.

Teacher: All alone?

Johnnie: Well, I helped him with it.

Teacher: If we breathe oxygen in the daytime, what do we breathe at night?

Gracie: Why, nitrogen, of course.

Teacher: At your age I could name all the Presidents — and in the proper order.

Student: Yes, but then there were only three or four of them.

Teacher, crossly: You've all been too noisy, so you'll have to stay after school.

Voice from back of the room: Give me liberty or give me death.

Teacher: Who said that?

Voice: Patrick Henry.

Teacher, severely: Johnny, I will ask your father to come and see me.

Johnny: You'll be sorry! He's a doctor and charges fifty dollars a visit!

One teacher to another, about the school pest: Not only is he the worst-behaved child in the school, he also has a perfect attendance record.

Teacher: Which three words are most frequently heard in the classroom?
Sam: I don't know.
Teacher: Correct.

Teacher: What is the first letter in the alphabet?
Johnnie: A.
Teacher: And what comes after A?
Johnnie: Er...all the other letters.

Lewis: I think our school must be haunted.
Lois: Where did you get that idea?
Lewis: Well I always hear people talking about the school spirit.

"What comes before six?" asked the kindergarten teacher.
"The Milkman," replied Susie.

Teacher (answering phone): You say Ben Bones has a bad cold and can't come to school? To whom am I speaking?
Voice: This is my father.

Teacher: Jasper, I can scarcely read your handwriting. You must learn to write more clearly.

Student: Oh, what's the use? If I wrote any better, you'd complain about my spelling.

CANNIBAL

Mrs. Cannibal to her husband: What are you doing?

Cannibal: I'm chasing a hunter around a tree.

Mrs. Cannibal: How many times must I tell you not to play with your food.

First cannibal: What is that book you're reading?

Second cannibal: It's called *How to Serve Your Fellow Man.*

"Tell me," said the missionary to the cannibal, "do you think religion has made any progress here?"

"Yes," answered the cannibal. "Now we only eat fishermen on Fridays."

Explorer to educated cannibal: Do you mean to tell me that you went to a university, and you still eat your enemies?"

Cannibal: Yes, but but now I use a knife and fork.

Missionary: Do you people know anything about religion?

Cannibal: We had a taste of it when the last missionary was here.

Missionary: Why are you looking at me like that?

Cannibal: I'm the food inspector.

Mother cannibal: What's baby up to?

Father cannibal: My waist.

First cannibal: Am I late to dinner?

Second cannibal: Yes, everybody's been eaten.

Mother cannibal to witch doctor: I'm worried about Junior, he wants to be a vegetarian.

Q: Why was the cannibal in a bad mood?

A: Because he was fed up with people.

Cannibal to victim: Silence! Food should be eaten and not heard!''

Cannibal Chief: What did you do for a living?

Victim: I was an associate editor.

Chief: Cheer up! Now you'll be an editor-in-chief."

Cannibal cook: A couple of eskimos have fallen into our hands, chief.

Chief: Splendid! I always wanted to try that frozen food.

Mother cannibal to child: How many times have I told you not to speak with someone in your mouth?

KIDS & ADULTS

Molly: Gee, I'm sure glad I wasn't born in France.

Sally: Why do you say that?

Molly: Because I can't speak a word of French.

Little boy: I've just swallowed a worm.

Friend: Hadn't you better take something for it?

Little boy: No, I'll let it starve.

Absent-minded professor: Lady, what are you doing in my bed?

Lady: Well, I like this bed. I like this neighborhood. I like this house, and anyway, I'm your wife.

Did you hear about the absent-minded professor who: Returned from lunch and saw a sign on his door, "Back in thirty minutes," and sat down to wait for himself?

Slammed his wife and kissed the door?

Got up and struck a match to see if he had blown out the candle?

Farmer: How do you treat a pig with a sore throat?

Vet: Apply Oinkment.

Waiter: How did you find your steak, sir?

Diner: Just by accident. I moved the baked potato and there it was.

Sign in a restaurant:
Don't laugh at our coffee. You may be old and weak some day too.

Prosecutor: Now tell the jury the truth please. Why did you kill your husband with a bow and arrow?

Defendant: I didn't want to wake the children.

My name is Cliff: Drop over someday!

Bob: Here's one for you. The Marines and Navy were playing basketball. All the Marines fouled out. Who would they put in?

Rob: I don't know.

Bob: The sub-marines.

Q: What do the Eskimos call their cows?

A: Eskimoos.

Crank caller: Is your refrigerator running?

Receiver: Yes.

Crank caller: You'd better go catch it!

Older Girl: Have you lived here all your life?

Sally: Not yet.

A high school boy took out of the library a book whose cover read *How to Hug* only to discover it was volume 7 of the encyclopedia.

Tim: I know something that occurs once in every minute, twice in every moment; but not once in a thousand years.

Jim: What's that?

Tim: The letter M.

Ron: Do you think if a man smashed a clock, he could be accused of killing time?

John: Not if the clock struck first.

Donna: Did you hear the astronauts found some bones on the moon?

Lisa: Oh, dear. Maybe the cow didn't make it after all.

Nick: Is it legal in this state for a man to marry his widow's sister?

Rick: Of course not. That man would be dead.

Smarty: Some months have thirty days, some thirty-one, but how many months have twenty-eight days?

Arty: February.

Smarty: Nope, all of them do.

Phil: Why did the chicken cross the road?

Bill: For fowl reasons.

Fred: If the green house is on the left side of the road, and if the red house is on the right side of the road, where is the white house?

Ned: How am I supposed to know?

Fred: Easy, it's in Washington.

Sam: What happens to girls who eat bullets?

Pam: Their hair grows out in bangs.

Judge: Name, occupation, and charge.

Prisoner: My name is Sparks; my occupation is electricity; the charge is battery.

Jim: Do you believe in fate?

Tim: I don't know. Why?

Jim: Well, didn't you ever wonder why famous men were all born on holidays?

Instructor: Watch where you're driving. You almost went off the road.

Student: I thought you were driving.

Two men were riding in a train for the first time. They had brought along some bananas for lunch. Just as they began to peel them they entered a dark tunnel.

"Have you eaten yours yet?" asked one of the men.

"No, why?"

"Well don't touch it. I took one bite and went blind."

Actor: Why did you quit the stage?

Comedian: Ill health.

Actor: What do you mean ill health?

Comedian: I made people sick.

Jane: Our next-door neighbors must be very poor.

Mother: What makes you say that?

Jane: You should have seen the fuss they made when their baby swallowed a penny.

Visitor in newspaper office: Where can I find the editor's office?

Boy: Go up the stairway marked "No Admittance" and walk through the door marked "Keep Out". Walk straight ahead until you get to the sign marked "Silence" and then yell for him.

Stern librarian: Please be quiet. The people near you can't read.

Small boy: Why, they ought to be ashamed of themselves! I've been able to read since I was six.

Doctor: Now, Ann, stick out your tongue.

Ann: Nothing doing. I got in trouble for doing that at home.

In the Egyptian room of the museum, Jack and Jill stopped before a mummy in a mummy case bearing a card which said: "2453 B.C.E.".

"What do you suppose it means?" whispered Jack.

"I don't know," replied Jill, "unless it's the license number of the car that hit him."

Kitty: Did you hear about the lady who married four times? Her first husband was a millionaire. Her second husband was a famous actor. Her third was a well-known minister, and her fourth was an undertaker.

Kat: Oh, I see. One for the money; two for the show; three to get ready; and four to go!

Waitress: I have stewed kidneys, boiled tongue, fried liver, and pig's feet.

Customer: I don't want to hear about your troubles. Just bring me some vegetable soup quickly.

Gloomy Gerty: Bald-headed men always seem to be so cheerful.

Jolly Jim: Why not? Nothing ever gets in their hair.

Ike: What would you say if your wife had quadruplets?

Spike: Four crying out loud.

"Ah Ha!" exclaimed the amateur detective at the scene of the crime, "this is worse than I thought. The window is broken on both sides!"

Ronnie: Is your new hunting horse well behaved?

Johnnie: He certainly is! He has such good manners that when we come to a fence, he stops and lets me go over first.

Hughie: Hey! Why are you wearing my raincoat?

Louie: You wouldn't want your best suit to get wet, would you?

Five-year-old Susan: Sit still, I'm trying to draw your picture.

Ellen: How's it coming?

Susan: Not so good. Guess I'll put a tail on and make it a dog.

Frank: And were you hurt in the fall, Hank?

Hank: Oh, no, the fall didn't harm me at all. It was hitting the ground that broke my leg.

Mechanic: The horn on your car must be broken.

Motorist: No, it's just indifferent.

Mechanic: What do you mean indifferent?

Motorist: It just doesn't give a hoot.

Burglar: The policemen are coming. Quick, jump out the window.

Accomplice: But we're on the thirteenth floor!

Burglar: This is no time to be superstitious.

A child expert says that children's clothes will stay clean for several days... if you keep them off the child.

Sergeant: So you're complaining about a little sand in your soup.

Private: Yes, sir.

Sergeant: Did you join the army to serve your country or to complain about food?

Private: I joined the army to serve my country, not to eat it.

John: My sister and I know every word in the dictionary.

Joe: What does egotistical mean?

John: That's one of the words my sister knows.

Benny: Just how broke are you?

Lenny: Well, right now all a pickpocket could get from me is practice.

Mr. Jones: They tell me your son is quite an author. Does he write for money?

Mr. Smith: Indeed yes... in every letter.

Andy: Have you forgotten that you owe me five dollars for those ice-skates?

Sandy: No, but give me time and I will.

Sam (opening lunch box at school): Aw, cream cheese and jelly sandwiches again.

Ralph: Why don't you tell your mother that you're tired of that kind?

Sam: What good will that do? I make my own lunch.

Jerry: Where did you get that black eye?

Terry: You see this door?

Jerry: Yes.

Terry: Well, I didn't.

A: How did you get that black eye?

B: I got hit by a guided muscle.

South Dakota is noted for very sudden changes of temperature. One summer day it got so hot that a field of popcorn started popping and really caused a flurry. The crows in the next field thought it was snowing and froze to death watching.

A: Did you come to my lollipop party?
B: No.
A: I thought there was a sucker missing!

Boy: Do you know that man over there? He's the meanest man I ever met.
Girl: Do you know who I am? I'm that man's daughter.
Boy: Do you know who I am?
Girl: No.
Boy: Thank goodness!

Doctor: How is the boy that swallowed the quarter?
Nurse: No change yet, sir.

There was a man who died from drinking varnish. It was an awful sight, but a beautiful finish.

Big boy: On my right hand was a lion, on my left was a tiger, in front and in back were wild elephants.

Little boy: What happened?

Big boy: The merry-go-round stopped.

Farmer: Quite a storm we had last night.

Neighbor: Yep, sure was.

Farmer: Damage your barn any?

Neighbor: Dunno, haven't found it yet.

Eskimo boy: What would you say if I told you I drove my dog sled five hundred miles over ice and snow just to tell you I love you?

Eskimo girl: I'd say that's a lot of "mush."

Red: Is it really bad luck to have a black cat follow you?

Fred: It depends whether you're a man or a mouse.

A Texas millionaire, walking into an automobile showroom: My wife is sick.

What do you have in the way of a get-well car?

A: Did anyone laugh when you fell on the ice?

B: No, but the ice made a few cracks.

A: Doctor, doctor, my son thinks he's Napoleon, and he just couldn't be!

B: Why not?

A: Because I am!

Ted: Have you ever studied a blotter?

Ed: No, why?

Ted: It's very absorbing.

Mike: What inventions have helped man get up in the world?

Ike: I don't know. Which ones?

Mike: The elevator, the escalator, and the alarm clock.

Mack: How was spaghetti invented?
Jack: I have no idea.
Mack: Some fellow used his noodle.

Sally (answering the phone): Hello.
Voice: Hello, is Boo there?
Sally: Boo who?
Voice: Don't cry, little girl. I must have the wrong number.

A hiker traveling the mountains of Arizona came upon an Indian sending smoke signals. When asked how big a fire he usually built, the Indian replied, "It all depends on whether it's a local call or a long-distance."

Alaskan: Our state is bigger than yours.
Texan: Won't be if it melts.

Rick: What kind of paper should I use when I make my kite?
Dick: How about flypaper?

Read in the will of a miserly millionaire: "...And to my dear brother Arnold, whom I promised to mention in my will, 'Hi there, Arnold!'"

Andy: Who makes up mystery and horror stories?

Randy: Ghost writers.

Sam: Why does the weather bureau name hurricanes after girls?

Sidney: Why?

Sam: If they named them after boys, they would be called himicanes.

Sally: Why were the Indians the first people in North America?

Brains: Because they had reservations.

Our enemies don't need missiles to destroy us. All they have to do is poison the glue on the backs of trading stamps.

Letter to weather bureau:

I thought you'd be interested in knowing that I shoveled three feet of "partly cloudy" from my porch.

Tim: Did you hear about the boy with gleam in his eye?

Jim: No, what about him?

Tim: Someone bumped him while he was brushing his teeth.

Frank: Yesterday I lit a cigarette with a twenty-dollar bill.

Hank: That was pretty extravagant, wasn't it?

Frank: Not really, it was a bill from my grocer, and I wasn't going to pay it anyway.

Passenger: Is this my train?

Conductor: No sir, it belongs to the railroad company.

Passenger: Don't be funny. I mean can I take this train to New York?

Conductor: No sir, it's much too heavy.

Romeo: Juliet, I'm burning with love for you.

Juliet: Come, now, Romeo, don't make a fuel of yourself.

Ted: Did you know you can't send mail to Washington?

Ned: No, why not?

Ted: Because he's dead. But you can send mail to Lincoln.

Ned: But he's dead too.

Ted: I know, but he left his Gettysburg Address.

Bill: He reminds me of Whistler's mother standing up.

Jill: What makes you say that?

Bill: He's off his rocker.

"My business is looking up," said the astronomer.

"Mine is just sew, sew," remarked the seamstress.

"Mine is growing," boasted the farmer.

Young agricultural student: Your methods of cultivation are terribly out of date. I'd be surprised if you could get ten pounds of apples from that tree.

Farmer: So would I. It's a peach tree.

An archeologist — a person whose career lies in ruins.

Coincide — what most people do when it rains.

Mosquito — A flying hypodermic needle.

Pasteurize — Too far to see.

Hatchet — What a hen does to an egg.

MORONS

Moron #1: Say that's a bad cut you've got on your forehead. How'd you get it?

Moron #2: I bit myself.

Moron #1: Oh come on! How could you bite yourself on the forehead.

Moron #2: I stood on a chair.

The little moron took a friend driving in the mountains. After awhile, his friend said, "Every time you race around one of those sharp curves, I get scared."

"Then why don't you do what I do?" the driving moron said. "What's that?" said the passenger.

"Close your eyes."

Red: Did you mark that place where the fishing was good?

Ted: Yes, I put an X on the side of the boat.

Red: That was stupid. What if you should take out another boat next time?

Moron: I'm sure my vegetable garden will be a success this year.

Neighbor: How can you tell so soon?

Moron: The chickens have tasted everything, and they were most enthusiastic.

Dope # 1: Did'ya see me walk in the door?

Dope # 2: Yes.

Dope # 1: Never saw me before in your life, did'ya?

Dope # 2: No.

Dope # 1: Then how did you know it was me?

Lenny: Guess what Danny did when he went to the movies?

Benny: What?

Lenny: He went to see *The Desert* and asked for two tickets in the shade.

Benny: That's nothing. Yesterday he stood in front of a mirror for half an hour trying to remember where he had seen himself before.

First Moron: Did you like the second act of the play?

Second Moron: I didn't see it. The program said 'Second Act two years later' and I couldn't wait.

Why did the moron drive off the cliff?
  To try out his air brakes.

Friend: Did you take a shower?
Moron: No, is there one missing?

First Moron: Where were you born?
Second Moron: In a hospital.
First Moron: No kidding, what was wrong with you?

Moron #1: Why are you painting the fence so fast?
Moron #2: I want to get the job done before I run out of paint.

Pam: Do you know how fishermen make their nets?
Sam: It's simple, Pam. They just take a handful of holes, sew them together, and there you are.

A: How can I cure myself of snoring? I snore so loud I wake myself.
B: Try sleeping in another room.

Moron #1: How can you find a rabbit that is lost in the woods?

Moron #2: Make like a bunny?

Moron #1: No, stupid, make a noise like a carrot.

Ann: Ouch! That water burned my hand.

Fran: You should have felt it before you put your hand in.

Moron #1: This match won't light.

Moron #2: What's the matter with it?

Moron #1: I don't know. It worked all right a minute ago.

ANIMALS

A man riding a horse passed a dog on the road.

"Good morning," said the dog.

"I didn't know dogs could talk," said the man.

"Neither did I," said the horse.

Penny: What kind of dog is that?

Benny: He's a police dog.

Penny: He sure doesn't look like one to me.

Benny: Of course not. He's in the Secret Service.

First dog: My name is Spot. What's yours?

Second dog: I'm not sure, but I think it's Down Boy.

Clancy: Say, did you know that I've got a baseball dog?

Nancy: What is a baseball dog?

Clancy: Well, he wears a muzzle, catches flies, chases fowls, and beats it for home when he sees the catcher coming.

Steven from the city was visiting a farm for the first time and was taken out to see the lambs. He finally got up enough courage to pet one.

"Why they're made out of blankets!" he exclaimed.

Doctor: What's the matter?

Kangaroo: I've been feeling jumpy lately.

Dolphin #1: What did you say when you bumped into that dolphin?

Dolphin #2: I just told him I didn't do it on porpoise.

Two flies were sitting on Robinson Crusoe's knee.

"Good-bye, now," said one, "I'll see you on Friday."

Joe: How do you describe a cow that has swallowed a bomb?

Jean: Abominable (A bomb in a bull).

Mama moth was surprised to see baby moth crying. "Stop that at once," she commanded. "This is the first time I've ever seen a moth bawl."

Buster: That your dog?

Rusty: Yes, he used to be a pointer, but my mother spoiled him.

Buster: How?

Rusty: She taught him it wasn't polite to point.

Mike: You know, my dog swallowed a flashlight yesterday.

Spike: Is he sick?

Mike: No, he spit it out last night, and now he's de-lighted.

A missionary was walking down a jungle path in the depths of Africa when he saw a lion coming toward him. He got down on his knees and bowed his head in prayer. When he looked up he saw the lion doing the same thing. The lion looked up and said:

"I don't know what you're doing, but I'm saying grace."

A: "This is dogwood."

B: "How can you tell?"

A: "By its bark."

Riddles

What did the beaver say to the tree?
"It was nice gnawing you!"

What did one clover say to the other clover
"Take me to your weeder."

What did the adding machine say to the clerk?
"You can count on me!"

What did the king cloud say to the rest of his clouds?
"I'm the one who should rain around here!"

What did the mother ghost say to the baby ghost?
"Fasten your sheet belt!"

What did the boy ghost say to Frankenstein?
"You'd better get out of here, or I'll tell my Mummy."

What did the bad lettuce say to the carrot?

"I've turned over a new leaf."

What did the rug say to the floor?

"Stick'em up! I got you covered."

What did the tie say to the hat?

"You go on ahead; I'll just hang around."

What did one candle ask the other candle?

"Are you going out tonight?"

What did the boy octopus say to the girl octopus?

"I want to hold your hand hand hand hand hand hand hand hand."

What did one ear say to the other?

"I didn't know we lived on the same block."

What did the cherry tree say to the farmer?

"Stop picking on me."

Why do skunks argue?

"Because they like to make a stink."

If a king likes to sit on gold, who likes to sit on silver?

"The Lone Ranger."

Why don't melons get married?

"Because they cantaloupe."

Why does an elephant have a trunk?

"Because he doesn't have a glove compartment."

Why is a heart like a policeman?

"They both have a regular beat."

What's the best thing to take when you're run down?

"The license number of the car that hit you."

What's white, blue, red, white, and blue?

"Betsy Ross making the flag without her glasses."

Why did the rabbit want the diamond?
   "Because it had fourteen carats."

Where can happiness always be found?
   "In a dictionary."

Why did the cookie cry?
   "Because its mother had been a wafer so long."

Why did the moron bring a spoon and some cream and sugar to the movie?
   "He heard it would be a serial."

What never asks questions but always has to be answered?
   "The telephone."

Why did the robber take a bath?
   "Because he wanted to make a clean getaway."

Why is a bride unlucky on her wedding day?
   "Because she isn't going to marry the best man."

Where is the smallest bridge in the world?

"On your nose."

Why does a hen lay eggs?

"Because if she let them drop, they would break."

What kind of coat is made without sleeves and put on wet?

"A coat of paint."

Why did the teacher marry the janitor?

"He swept her off her feet."

What do you call a hundred-year old watch dog?

"An oldtimer."

When was beef the highest?

"When the cow jumped over the moon."

What question can you never answer with yes?

"Are you asleep?"

What did the painter say to the wall?

"One more crack like that, and I'll plaster you."

Why did the man throw his pants out the window?

"He heard a boy yelling 'free press.'"

Have you heard the joke about the sidewalk?

"It's all over town."

What did the man put in the twenty-pound barrel to make it weigh only ten pounds?

A hole.

When a little boy is spanked first by his father, then by his mother, who hurts the most?

"The little boy."

How many wives is a man given by the minister in the marriage service?

"Sixteen: four better; four worse; four richer; four poorer."

What makes a baker like a bank robber?
"They always have their hands in the dough."

What part of a fish weighs the most?
"The scales."

What kind of boats do vampires like?
"Blood vessels."

How do sailors get their clothes clean?
They throw them overboard and then they are washed ashore."

What holds up a train?
"Train robbers."

Why did the boy put hay in his bed each night?
"He wanted to feed his night-mare."

What did Batman say when he picked up the hot line?
"Ouch!"

What do you get when you cross a duck with a fire?

"A fire quacker."

If the father bull was standing up and the baby bull was lying down, what was the mother bull doing?

"There are no mother bulls."

Why didn't they play cards on Noah's Ark?

"Because Noah sat on the deck."

What is a duck called that has a straight A report card?

"A wise quacker."

Why didn't the baby moth cry when his mother spanked him?

"Everyone knows you can't make a moth bawl."

What is the best thing to make in a hurry?

"Haste."

What is the keynote of good manners?

"B Natural."

What are the spooks in the Navy called?
"The Ghost Guard."

What always weighs the same no matter what size it is?
"A hole."

What word is usually pronounced wrong even by the most prominent of scholars?
"Wrong, of course."

What kind of shoes are made of banana skins?
"Slippers."

What geometrical figure represents a lost parrot?
"A Polygone (Polly gone)."

What liquid is like the load a freight ship carries?
"Gasoline, because it makes the car go."

When is spanking like a hat?
  "When it is felt."

Why is Sunday the strongest day?
  "Because all the others are week-days."

What is the spooks' defense system called?
  "The Ghost Guard."

How do you know "S" is mean?
  "Because it makes cream scream."

How do you make anti-freeze?
  "Steal her blanket."

Why did the basketball player flood the gym?
  "Because the coach asked him to come in as a sub."

Why did the three pigs leave home?

"They thought their father was an awful boar."

Why is the letter E like London?

"Because it is the capital of England."

Why did the little boy sleep on the chandelier?

"Because he was a light sleeper."

Why is an icy sidewalk like music?

"If you don't see sharp, you'll be flat."

What has nothing left but nose when it loses an eye?

"Noise."

Why is a watermelon filled with water?

"Because it is planted in the spring."

What do you call a frightened seadiver?
   "Chicken of the sea."

If all the people in the U.S. owned pink cars, what would the country be called?
   "A pink carnation."

If Washington's wife went to Washington while Washington's wash women washed Washington's work clothes, how many "W's" are there in all?
   "There are no 'W's' in all. None."

What did the baby porcupine say when he backed into a cactus?
   "Is that you, Ma?"

Why do movie stars keep cool?
   "Because they have so many fans."

Why is doing nothing so tiring?
   "Because you can't stop and rest."

What is the best way to keep fish from smelling?
   "Cut off their noses."

Why is baseball like a cake?

"They both depend on the batter."

Why did the farmer name his pig Ink?

"Because he was always running out of his pen."

What did the lightning bug say as he was leaving?

"Got to glow now."

Why is an ice-cream cone like a horse?

"The more you lick it the faster it goes."

How do you know that "B" is hot?

"Because it makes oil boil."